HOW TO ORGANIZE YOUR CLASSROOM

by Katherine Ruggieri

Fearon Teacher Aids
A Division of Frank Schaffer Publications, Inc.

To Mary Ruggieri, who through her commitment, wisdom, and sincerity,
has touched the lives of many, including mine.

Award-winning photojournalist Bruce Hazelton traveled to Poulsbo, Washington to
photograph Katherine Ruggieri and students from Suquamish Elementary School. Fearon
Teacher Aids would like to thank the following students for their joyful
participation—(front row, left to right:) Taylor Rapavy, John Stiffler, Sarah Gray, Teyah Ruggieri,
Meghan O'Hara, Jenna Shasky, Natalie Journey, Alex Vidal, (back row) Allen Jaqua,
Peter Crabtree, Britt Seaberg, Claire Watson, Jonah Bomgaars, Christopher Dalton,
Christopher Hall, Kiah VandePutte, Christine Parker, Erika Scott, Elise Thrasher—and
Julia Boubel and Sam Wenberg (not pictured).

Senior Editor: Kristin Eclov

Editor: Janet Barker

Copy Editor: Christine Hood

Photographer: Bruce Hazelton

Cover and Interior Design: Rose Sheifer Graphic Productions

Fearon Teacher Aids products were formerly manufactured and distributed by
American Teaching Aids, Inc., a subsidiary of Silver Burdett Ginn, and are now
manufactured and distributed by Frank Schaffer Publications, Inc. FEARON,
FEARON TEACHER AIDS, and the FEARON balloon logo are marks used under
license from Simon & Schuster, Inc.

© Fearon Teacher Aids
A Division of Frank Schaffer Publications, Inc.
23740 Hawthorne Boulevard
Torrance, CA 90505-5927

FE7972

ISBN 0-7682-0050-4

CONTENTS

Introduction: iv

Ch. 1: Organizing Your Environment 1
　Desk Arrangement 1
　Teacher's Desk 3
　Bulletin Boards. 3
　Creating Board Space. 5
　Whiteboards and Chalkboards 6
　Books and Bookshelves 7
　Cupboards and Storage Space 9
　Classroom Supplies. 10
　Classroom Shopping List 11

Ch. 2: Organizing Routines and Rituals 12
　Attendance 12
　Coats and Backpacks 14
　Lining Up 14
　Recess Equipment. 16
　Lunches 17
　Sharing. 18
　Classroom Helpers 21
　Emergency Drills 22
　Assemblies 24
　Bathroom Use 25
　Daily Schedules 27
　Field Trips 29
　Field Trip Volunteer Form 30
　Classroom Management 31

Ch. 3: Organizing Math 33
　Manipulatives 33
　Content 34
　Products. 36
　Evaluation 37

Ch. 4: Organizing Reading. 39
　Content Ideas. 39
　Reading Groups 41
　Materials 43

**Ch. 5: Organizing Language Arts
　and Spelling.** 45
　Language Arts Ideas 45
　Spelling Ideas. 48

Ch. 6: Organizing Student Work 51
　Passing Out and Collecting
　　Student Assignments. 51
　Work to Be Saved or Shared 53
　Giving Feedback on Student Work ... 55
　Homework Notice 56

Ch. 7: Organizing Communication 57
　Communicating with Students 58
　Communicating with
　　Students' Parents 60
　Communicating with Staff 62

Ch. 8: Organizing Paperwork 63
　Filing. 63
　Absent Work 65
　Makeup Assignments 66

A Final Note 67

INTRODUCTION

As an elementary school teacher, you spend a significant portion of your waking hours in the classroom. Your classroom is much more than simply a space that houses you, it's your home for eight hours a day. As a teacher, you're the head of a school family and the classroom is where you live. In your classroom space, you and your students create an academic life together. Your classroom reflects your attitude toward the value and purpose of education. It reveals how you feel about your students and your job as a teacher. Your classroom is a reflection of who you are professionally.

Throughout the school year, children and adults will enter your class and develop an instant impression. Will your classroom suggest, "You are welcome here," "Kids are important," and "Learning is what we are about"? Or, will the message be, "Sit down and be quiet," "I am not happy here," and "I don't know what I am doing and I only pray I'll make it through the day"? Every item you choose to display in your classroom provides a clue—from the words pinned to the walls, to the colors, pictures, and decorations you select. Even something as seemingly insignificant as where you place your desk reflects your attitude about teaching.

Although the concept of organization is simple, becoming organized often takes years of experience. It includes basic decisions such as where you place pencils and where to put your desk, to the most intricate curriculum planning. *How to Organize Your Classroom* will help you shave years off that process by offering dozens of easy-to-implement, practical, organizing tips.

How to Organize Your Classroom is divided into eight chapters. Each section targets a specific area, such as how to store supplies, how to organize field trips, and how to communicate with parents. Use the book as a quick reference for idea-gathering or long-term planning.

Since no two children are alike and no two days are the same, there's little predictability in teaching, a vocation filled with fascinating and unique beings who require endless degrees of flexibility and creativity. Whether you've just been assigned your first classroom, or you've been teaching for 20 years, *How to Organize Your Classroom* will help you spend less time on tedious classroom management and more time doing what you do best—touching the hearts and minds of children.

Katherine Ruggieri

Organizing Your Environment

Your classroom environment is everything that surrounds you—from bulletin boards to lunch cards. Each item needs to be well thought out and organized in order to create a comfortable, efficient classroom environment.

Desk Arrangement

Student desks should be oriented around the most frequently used chalk or whiteboard. Desks may directly face the board or be perpendicular to it. Position desks so that children are able to easily pay attention. When arranging desks, consider students' age. Some children prefer to have their own space. For example, to a first grader, having his or her own desk is a new and exciting passage which says, "Now, I'm a big kid." He or she will likely be very possessive of his or her new space. Student desk arrangement reflects your expectations of how students will interact with each other. Decide how much communication you want and arrange desks accordingly.

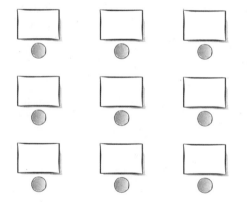

 Student desks can be organized in rows. This formation will limit student communication. However, this arrangement is valuable for talkative classes. Another advantage is that students can easily pair up during cooperative learning by having alternate rows move desks toward a partner in a stationary row.

 To encourage teamwork, organize student desks in tables or groups. This arrangement encourages relaxed communication. Usually a group of three to five students is best. A group of more than five usually ends up functioning as two smaller groups. Tables or groups can earn points or privileges, such as first out to recess, for appropriate behavior.

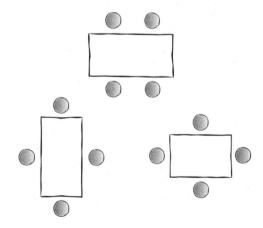

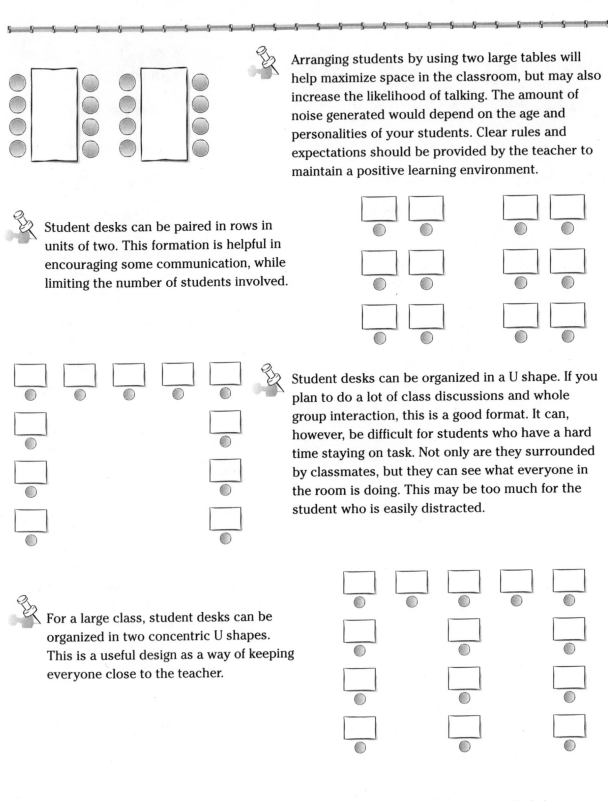

Arranging students by using two large tables will help maximize space in the classroom, but may also increase the likelihood of talking. The amount of noise generated would depend on the age and personalities of your students. Clear rules and expectations should be provided by the teacher to maintain a positive learning environment.

Student desks can be paired in rows in units of two. This formation is helpful in encouraging some communication, while limiting the number of students involved.

Student desks can be organized in a U shape. If you plan to do a lot of class discussions and whole group interaction, this is a good format. It can, however, be difficult for students who have a hard time staying on task. Not only are they surrounded by classmates, but they can see what everyone in the room is doing. This may be too much for the student who is easily distracted.

For a large class, student desks can be organized in two concentric U shapes. This is a useful design as a way of keeping everyone close to the teacher.

It is not necessary to keep student desks in the same formation all year. If you find that a certain arrangement is not working for you, change it. If you find one that works, keep it. Whatever desk formation you choose, change individual seating within the formation every two to four weeks to allow students to see new faces and hear new ideas. Students can take their desks with them to their new spot, or just take their belongings and place them in a new desk.

Teacher's Desk

The teacher's desk should be placed in a way that best helps you function efficiently in the classroom. If you plan to sit at your desk and interact with students, then place your desk where you have the best view. Many teachers place their desk at the side or the back of the room. This placement reflects the teacher's role as a guide who participates in learning, rather than one who directs. The placement of the teacher's desk will either invite student access or limit it. It is not necessary to allow student access to your desk in order to be a friendly and open teacher.

Bulletin Boards

 Bulletin boards are one of the most visible items in the room. Avoid crowded or cluttered bulletin boards because they can be intimidating and are often overlooked. They do not convey the sense of a well-organized teacher.

 Avoid leaving a bulletin board blank, unless you or the children are in the process of designing it. If you have nothing to display, cover it with bright wrapping paper and display student work or student photographs.

 Decide whether you want bulletin boards to be permanent or changed periodically. If you have several boards, you may want some to change and some to stay the same. The permanent ones can be in the less accessible places.

Bulletin boards can be covered with a variety of materials such as butcher paper, wrapping paper, or wallpaper. Cloth also makes a nice backing for bulletin boards and can be stapled into place, just like paper. If you plan to leave the covering on between board changes, use something that will wear well. A nonseasonal color is best if you plan to leave it on a long time.

 Borders used on a bulletin board can make it look more finished. Borders can be purchased or handcrafted by you or your students using narrow strips of butcher paper. If you use a seasonal border, be sure to change it when the season ends.

 The shape of the board need not confine you. You can hang large sheets of covering to drape, extend, and reshape the edges of the board.

Carefully choose colors when planning a bulletin board. Use calming colors whenever possible. Be careful of bright, bold colors. Vibrant colors tend to agitate young children. Try using cool colors to create a peaceful mood. Avoid placing large portions of primary colors on primary colors.

 Words and messages should contrast from the rest of the bulletin board. Letter size should be large enough to view from across the room.

 If you want students to design or assemble a bulletin board, be sure the canvas is easily accessible. Avoid having students stand on a chair or stool to reach the top of the board.

 Student work can be displayed on bulletin boards and changed as subjects expand. Be sure each student's name can be seen on the displayed work. A time-saving step is to create reusable nameplates out of white index cards to hang near students' work. Laminate them for durability.

 When displaying student work on a long-term basis, it's best to follow a specific format. For example, you may choose to spotlight students' writing, their best work of the week, or artwork. For a long-term display, each student should have his or her own spot. This will make student work easier to find—for them and for you. Attach their work to the bulletin board with pushpins; this provides a way to add future papers. Punch holes in the upper corners of the work (you may have to punch several overlapping holes), then slip the hole over the pushpin. This enables you to store the displayed work on the bulletin board throughout the year by adding each new piece to the top. At the end of the year, you have a ready-made packet of work to send home.

 If you plan to reuse a bulletin board display in the future, store all its pieces together in a large resealable bag. Letters, pictures, and borders can all be stored together to avoid having to reassemble the next time you use the display.

 Your bulletin boards should reflect the high-quality standards you require of your students. Correct spelling and neatness are a must.

Creating Board Space

If you find yourself in a classroom without display space, use materials to cover the walls to create the illusion of bulletin boards.

 Display student work on doors and windows. First, cover space with butcher paper, then frame using borders.

 Tack, tape, or pin paper directly to walls.

 Mount corkboard, purchased in bulk at a hardware supply store, to the walls.

 Attach lightweight rugs to the wall to create a warm and cozy feeling.

Whiteboards and Chalkboards

Whiteboards and chalkboards are important messengers of information. Be sure to keep them clean and uncluttered. Clean the board and ledge as often as necessary to avoid streaks and an accumulation of chalk or marker dust. Be cautious of children who may have dust allergies. When erasing a large area, use two erasers. Hold one in each hand and do a windshield wiper movement. This will make a tedious task more fun while amusing your students at the same time.

 If you write your daily schedule on the board, always write it in the same spot each day. This will help children get into the habit of checking for information.

 To record names of students who have missing homework or overdue library books, and to display other notices, create a "business box." Use colored tape or a paper border to create a square on the chalkboard or whiteboard. The information can then be written in the "business box." Students will get in the habit of checking for their names.

 Don't use your board to stick up a lot of reminder notes. This will make the space look very busy, and for some children it will be distracting. A selected number of reminder notes can be used. Place reminders next to subject areas, such as bus notes near the exit, lunch notes near the lunch lineup area, and private notes in your private file.

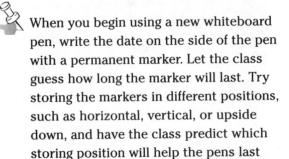 When you begin using a new whiteboard pen, write the date on the side of the pen with a permanent marker. Let the class guess how long the marker will last. Try storing the markers in different positions, such as horizontal, vertical, or upside down, and have the class predict which storing position will help the pens last longest.

Books and Bookshelves

The generous presence and easy availability of colorful and attractive books in the classroom will encourage children to read. Design a comfortable reading area near the books where students can relax and enjoy reading. A small rug or individual carpet square can define a reading area. An appliance box, beanbag chair, or even a canoe lined with pillows make a cozy reading nook.

 All books should be clearly labeled with your name or the school name and room number. Whenever possible, identification should be in the same spot in every book.

 Students must have a clear understanding of your expectations for the care and handling of books. Any book that is torn or soiled should be reported to you so it can be repaired, replaced, or taken out of circulation. Circulating books that are in poor condition decreases a child's respect for them.

 Permit students to check out some of the classroom books to take home. Place each book in a large resealable bag with a library check-out card. Students sign the card, leave it in the appointed spot, and take the book home in the resealable bag.

One book for one night is a good policy for young children.

 Letting children take home a book of their choice helps encourage them to read independently. Although this practice may increase the risk of losing a few books to damage or misplacement, it is well worth the risk.

 Use a magazine or book display rack to encourage students to read. Display covers whenever possible as they are specifically designed to excite a child's interest. Books standing up on top of a low bookshelf is a good way to show off book covers.

 Display books in some meaningful order rather than putting them out randomly. Group them according to topic, size, or type of book, such as magazine, hardback, or paperback. This helps students focus on what they are looking for and also sends the message that books are valuable and worth caring for.

 If no shelves are available, several wide-mouthed plastic baskets can be used to group books together. This kind of storage also permits you to arrange the books so that many covers are visible.

Offer books written in a variety of reading levels and on many different topics.

 Periodically rotate books, storing out-of-circulation materials in the cupboard for a few weeks. Next time you bring them out, they'll be seen with fresh eyes.

 No matter what level students you have, it's important to have as many reference books as you can beg, borrow, or buy. Include dictionaries, atlases, encyclopedias, thesauruses, and how-to books.

 Let students see you reading and using books. Many schools designate a specific time for sustained reading each day. Model the joy of reading by reading yourself. If your school doesn't have a school-wide sustained reading period, introduce one to your class. Reading aloud 15 minutes a day motivates students to read on their own.

 Books that students do not need access to can be placed out of the central classroom area, such as inside cupboards or on high shelves. Place your own reference books near your desk, with those you use most at eye level.

 Have a selection of books available for parents. Include educational magazines, parenting books, and materials that address child development. Also include books parents might enjoy reading to their children. To keep track of the books, have a readily visible sign-out sheet with spaces for parents to write their names, book titles, and the date.

 Bookshelves can be used as dividers to create different areas within the classroom. Be sure students are still visible to you—no matter where they are in the room. Low bookshelves work best as dividers— they don't block your view, and there is less risk of them accidentally toppling over.

 If a bookshelf is too tall for your students, consider removing the shelves and turning the bookshelf on its side. Place books in crates and baskets.

 If you live in an earthquake area, bookcases must be carefully bolted to the wall.

Cupboards and Storage Space

Plan your use of cupboard and storage space carefully. These spaces can be helpful to you, and should not be seen as just a place to stash unwanted items.

 First, draw out a storage plan to visualize your ideas. This makes it easy to make changes, and will save moving things twice.

 Anything you don't have to store, don't. Donate, dump, or deliver it to someone who wants it, needs it, or has room for it.

 Keep a box in one of your cupboards labeled "Miscellaneous Items." This will save you from fretting over where to put small items that seem to have no specific home.

 Have a "Transition Box" for items that you think you may want to discard, but are not quite sure yet. Leave the items in the box until you are sure you will not need them. Often the items in the box lose their importance and can be happily discarded.

 Anything that looks cluttered should be stored behind doors to avoid visual overload. Label cupboards on the outside or on the edge of the shelf. You may think you will remember how you have organized them, but you may not. For storage areas that children will be accessing, the labels should be on the outside of the cupboard in large and clearly understood letters. This will cut down on rummaging.

 Whenever possible, store items near where you will need them. Use high or out-of-reach cupboards for materials students do not need access to.

 Try to place related items together. This will save you time when you are putting together projects and activities.

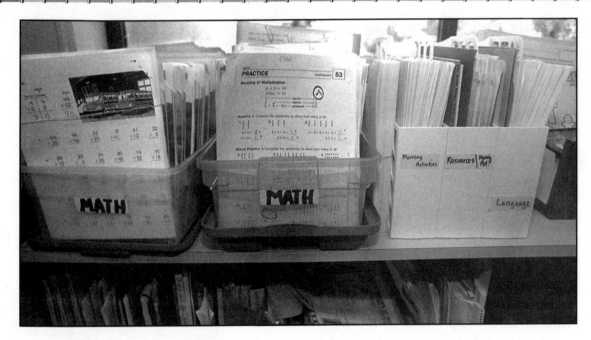

 If you live in an earthquake area, be careful of how you fill cupboards. Heavy items on high shelves can be dangerous. If your school doesn't provide door latches, place a stick or child-safety latch through the handles to prevent doors from opening.

 Use tall cupboard spaces, such as those designed for hanging coats, to store large posters. (Although many classrooms provide large shallow drawers for such posters, piling them one on top of the other makes them very impractical to use. Such a stack becomes too heavy to sort through.) In the tall closet, stand the posters on end and use pieces of tagboard as dividers. Label the outer edge of the tagboard with a computer address label folded lengthwise and attach it to the front and back for double visibility.

 If you are short on storage space, use large plastic tubs available at variety and hardware stores. Tubs can be stacked in a corner and labeled for easy access. Do not mix items. Each tub should contain only related items. Tubs can be given a general subject label such as "Math," or a more specific title such as "Place Value." Be specific—in the long run it will save you time.

Classroom Supplies

Post a reproducible shopping list, such as that on page 11, to the inside of a cupboard. As supplies run out and new items are needed, simply check off the depleted items. As needs expand, add new items to the list. Before purchasing supplies, check to see if items are available through the district.

CLASSROOM SHOPPING LIST

OTHER ITEMS

1. Paper clips—large and small
2. Pens—ballpoint, felt-tip, various colors
3. Pencils—colored and regular No. 2 leads
4. Erasers—pencil cap and rectangular pink
5. Writing paper
6. Construction paper—all colors
7. Drawing paper—white and newsprint,
8. Glue—both liquid and stick
9. Tape—masking (wide) and clear
10. Markers—permanent and nonpermanent
11. More markers—enough to fill a container
12. Crayons—enough to fill a container forstudent use
13. Rulers and yardsticks/metersticks—a dozen for class use
14. Bandages—more than you think you'll need
15. Stickers—positive incentives
16. Whiteboard markers—various colors
17. Chalk—multicolored
18. Overhead projector pens—all size, multicolored
19. Rubber bands—various sizes
20. Hole punchers—individual and three-hole
21. Staplers—two, good quality for student use
22. Staples
23. Clipboards
24. Individual slates

25. _____
26. _____
27. _____
28. _____
29. _____
30. _____
31. _____
32. _____

CHAPTER TWO

Organizing Routines and Rituals

Attendance

Most schools require the classroom teacher to take attendance each day. The obvious goal of taking attendance is to record, for both the office and parents, who is absent. Also, state funding is often tied in to student attendance. The less obvious, yet more important, goal of taking attendance is to purposefully validate each student's presence in your classroom. Students need to know that you are aware of them and pleased that they are present.

Taking attendance should not be a time-consuming task. It should take no more than five to seven minutes. Any more than this and it becomes a waste of time. If you find that your attendance-taking routine is taking more time than it should, consider changing it.

Depending on the age of your students, there are many ways attendance can be taken. You can make this a learning activity that involves the whole class or a quick check that involves just a few people. For older students, a quick check may be all the time you have. Try to involve the whole class if you have young students. Taking role offers an opportunity to practice listening skills.

 Read names from the attendance sheet out loud and have students stand when they hear their names.

 Read names from the attendance sheet out loud and have students stand when they hear the name of the person sitting next to them.

 Read names from the attendance sheet out loud and have students respond with a certain word relating to a classroom activity. For example, if you have been studying nouns, students could respond with a noun when they hear their names. Following a unit on food groups, students could respond with an item from a particular food group when their names are read.

 Read names from the attendance sheet out loud and have students turn in homework when their names are read.

"**R**outines and rituals" are the many activities that are done day after day and week after week in your classroom. They're not the interesting units and creative lessons that you teach your students. They're not the beautiful works of art or unique sculptures that your students share on parent night. Rather, routines and rituals are the nuts and bolts of classroom life. They include attendance, where to store coats, lining up, recess equipment, lunches, sharing, classroom helpers, fire drills, assemblies, bathroom use, daily schedules, field trips, and classroom management.

There are many ways of taking student attendance without involving the whole class. One way is to write each student's name on a plastic milk bottle cap and glue a magnet to the back of it. Place the magnetic caps on the chalkboard or whiteboard near the ledge. Draw a smiley face on the board above where the magnets are to be placed. As students arrive at school, have them move their magnet up to the smiley face. You can quickly see who is absent by noticing which magnets remain at the ledge. Be sure to do a quick check to see if students are really absent or have just forgotten to move their magnets.

Have a student read the names from the attendance sheet out loud and have students stand when they hear their names. Allow different students to be in charge of reading the names every day.

Another way is to hang a clothesline in the classroom. Write students' names on clothespins. As students come in, have them remove their names from the clothesline and drop them into a nearby basket labeled "Attendance" or "I'm Here." The clothespins of absent students will remain on the clothesline. At the end of school day, replace clothespins for the next day. The clothesline must be low enough for students to reach, but should not be placed where they're apt to walk into it.

Have a hat with a large brim turned upside down near the classroom door. Attach clothespins (label each pin with a student's name) around the hat brim. As students walk into the classroom have them remove their clothespins and drop them into the bowl of the hat.

For a student-made element, give each student a 4" x 2" (10 cm x 5 cm) piece of tagboard. Using the tagboard, have them create self-portraits, from head to toe. Put out two baskets—one labeled, "Home," and the other labeled, "School." Place all student tagboard portraits in the "Home" basket. As students enter the classroom, have them place their portraits in the "School" basket.

Coats and Backpacks

Your classroom may or may not have coat hooks for students to use. If your classroom does have them, don't feel obligated to use them if they aren't convenient. Coats can be kept on the back of student chairs. This makes them handy for recess or emergency drill purposes. The shoulders of the coats should be hung over the chair back. If the chair back has a space in it, loop the sleeves around the chair frame. This keeps coats from hanging on the floor. If lice is a problem in your area be sure coats are not hung together. Lice will spread quickly.

Consider using coat hooks for backpacks. Have students get into the routine of hanging backpacks up as soon as they walk into class. Homework and other items that need to be turned in should be removed from the packs prior to the day's first lesson to avoid unnecessary disruption.

Lining Up

Early in the school year, state the purpose of proper line behavior and explain exactly what your expectations are. Help students recognize the importance of being able to move efficiently through the school from one place to another. State clearly what you expect from your students when they are in line. Having an easy-to-remember checklist may help them get ready quickly. When possible, give choices. For example, hands may be in one of three places—clasped in front, at their sides, or clasped in back.

Depending on your students' age, they may need to practice walking in line. Allow time to accomplish this early in the year.

Do not allow your students to adopt a casual attitude toward line behavior. Explain that line etiquette is important in case of an emergency. It's sometimes thought that a casual, talkative line represents a high level of friendship and rapport between students and the teacher. In actuality, it represents a lack of manners and respect and can be annoying to those around you. In order to convince your students that you will follow up on your pre-set expectations for in-line behavior, wait until your line is completely quiet before leaving the classroom. At the beginning of the year you may have to allow extra time for this waiting period while students learn to be quiet.

 Praise your students often for their orderly line behavior. By pointing out the rules that were followed, you are reinforcing good behavior.

If your students are walking in line and become disruptive, stop and wait for them

 to refocus. Encourage students to remind each other to be quiet by silently putting their index fingers across their lips.

If possible, alternate where you walk in line with your students. For younger students you may find it necessary to walk in front of the line most of the time, but fall back occasionally to be near the middle of the line. With older students, you can walk in the back of the line. This gives you a different perspective and it allows students to feel that you are confident of their abilities.

 You may include the job of line leader in your classroom job list. The line leader should be at the head of the line whenever your class lines up. It is the student's responsibility to be a quiet leader and set a good example. If line leaders do not fulfill their duties, they should be relieved of their job temporarily. Offer them another chance later in the day.

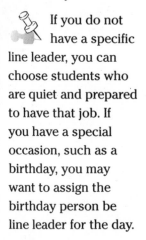 If you do not have a specific line leader, you can choose students who are quiet and prepared to have that job. If you have a special occasion, such as a birthday, you may want to assign the birthday person be line leader for the day.

Some districts don't allow boys and girls to be segregated in different lines. Be aware of district guidelines and follow them, regardless of your personal preference.

Recess Equipment

If you keep recess equipment in your classroom, provide one particular area where it's always stored. A large box or tub is ideal for this purpose. Use a permanent marker to label recess equipment, writing your room number in several spots.

Have students be responsible for keeping track of recess equipment. If a student takes an item out to recess, it is his or her responsibility to bring it back to the classroom. Stating this policy is generally all you'll need for students to be responsible for the equipment. However, if equipment begins to disappear, you'll have to create a formal check-out system. Be warned that such systems can be time-consuming and laborious and should be avoided, if at all possible.

To create a formal recess equipment check-out system you'll need a clipboard, a check-out paper, and a pencil or pen attached to the clipboard with a string. Your check-out paper should list every item available for recess check-out. These items can be listed down the left margin. Next to each item should be two squares. The first square is for students to write their initials in when taking a piece of recess equipment. The second square is for students to write their initials in when the equipment is returned.

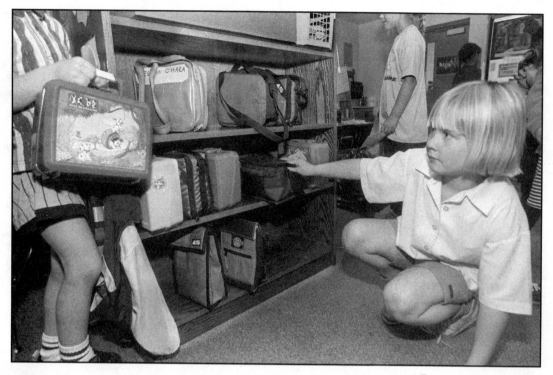

Lunches

Have students remove lunch boxes and bags from their backpacks upon arrival, so that any leaks or spills will be discovered early.

 Keep a roll of absorbent paper towels on hand in case a lunch-box leak is discovered. Have students open their lunch boxes in the class sink and remove any wet or leaking items. If you don't have a class sink, keep a dish-washing tub handy for lunch box cleanup. Store the paper-towel roll in the tub and tuck them away until both are needed.

 Make sure all lunch boxes and bags are clearly labeled with first and last names. Lunches can be placed on a shelf or counter. Don't store them in a sunny spot where boxes will warm up and cause food to spoil.

 Another idea is to directly place lunches in a laundry basket. At lunchtime, have monitors carry the distinctively-labeled basket to the lunch area. At the end of the

lunch period, children will place their bags and boxes in the basket and the lunch monitors will bring it back to class. If lunch cards need to be passed out, have a volunteer (depending on the age of your students) pass them out each day.

 Use a wall chart with pockets to store lunch cards so students can be responsible for their own cards. Number the cards so they can be found easily and you can tell if some are missing. Lunch cards can also be stored in students' cubbyholes or mailboxes.

 When numbering lunch cards have each student learn and remember his or her own number. Write students' numbers on their name tags to help them remember. Store the cards in numerical order, assigning a student the task of sequencing numbers.

Sharing

 Play an alphabet game while passing out lunch cards. Start with any letter in the alphabet and have students whose names (first or last) start with that letter stand up to receive their cards. Then students whose names begin with the next letter in the alphabet stand and retrieve their card, and so on.

 Sing a number song while passing out the lunch cards such as, "One, two, buckle my shoe; three four, shut the door . . .," or "One little, two little, three little lunch cards . . ." (to the tune of "One Little Indian").

 Streamline lunch procedures as much as you can so your students will know the routine. This will especially help on hectic days. Your students will know what to expect and will be able to work quickly.

Most students—no matter what their ages—enjoy being in the spotlight, if only for a few moments. If your schedule allows, have sharing time each day. Decide if you want to encourage spontaneous sharing or just one share day per child each week. During sharing, have the student who will be sharing sit in front of the class on a stool or chair. Require that all other students listen attentively. This is an important skill for students to practice and it helps build positive interpersonal relationships. When the student who is sharing finishes, have him or her ask the class for any questions or comments. Consider writing on cue cards three standard prompt questions, utilizing several of the five *who, what, when, why,* and *where* inquiries.

If the student sharing is feeling shy or embarrassed about being in front of the class, he or she may need your initial support. To ease nerves, ask the student a few easy questions. Sometimes just standing next to a child can be a confidence booster.

Make sharing optional. Students should not be forced to share. Often, students can be encouraged and convinced to share, but if not, they should be allowed to listen to others. Some students may be slow to start sharing and may need your verbal assistance. Your dialogue may go something like this:

Teacher: *"What do you have to share today?"*

Student: *"A bunny."*

Teacher: *"Is your bunny real?"*

Student: *"No."*

Teacher: *"Does your bunny have a name?"*

Student: *"I don't know. Fuzzy, I think."*

Teacher: *"Where did you get your bunny?"*

Student: *"From my grandma."*

Teacher: *"Do you have anything else you want to tell us?"*

Student: *"No."*

Don't be discouraged by these kinds of interactions. Students benefit from sharing in front of others, no matter what form it takes. As they continue to share, their comfort level will grow and you'll be able to take a smaller role in their sharing.

You may have some students who love to share. They may claim the stage and ramble as long as they're allowed. For this student sharing time can be an opportunity to practice focusing on one point and sticking to the topic. You may need to gracefully enforce a time limit. The following comments can be used to wrap up this student's sharing:

- *"Tell us one more thing, and then we will have questions."*

- *"What a wonderful story. Thanks for sharing it."*

- *"Your time is up, if you want to leave time for questions."*

Establish a "museum" in your classroom to display shared items. The museum can be a tub, box lid, or spot on a table. Make a portable museum by writing *museum* on a large piece of tagboard and placing it on top of a table or counter. Allow students to place their shared items in the museum for the day. Students should tell the class whether the object is for "touching" or "just looking at with your eyes" before placing it in the museum.

 Discuss with your students the kind of items that may not be shared. Items not permissible would include anything not allowed at school, such as violent, gross, highly valuable, and breakable materials.

 Students can be encouraged to bring in items that go along with classroom topics.

Some possibilities include:
- Items of a particular color
- Items that begin with a certain letter
- Common nouns
- Transportation
- Student-crafted items
- Personally historic, such as baby items
- Items from foreign countries
- Items with moving parts
- Items made from certain materials such as cotton or plastic.

 If students want to share a pet or person be sure to have them check with you beforehand. Inquire about possible student allergies before allowing a pet to visit. If students touch the animal, be sure to have moist hand wipes available for hand-cleaning.

When students are finished sharing, encourage them to ask the class if there are any questions or comments. Allow only two questions or comments from the class.

Classroom Helpers

Using student helpers is a great way to involve everyone in the responsibilities of classroom life. Students love being helpers and generally take the job very seriously.

Classroom helpers need to reflect your management style. Decide which jobs you want students to do and which jobs you prefer to do yourself. This will vary depending on the age of your students. Some job possibilities include:

JOB	DESCRIPTION
Paper passer	passes out papers to students
Messenger	carries paperwork to office
Color guard	leads class in flag salute
Inspector	checks on classroom clean up
Line leader	leads line in and out of class
Recess monitor	checks to make sure equipment is returned
Light monitor	turns out lights when class leaves
Librarian	straightens classroom books
Attendance taker	takes attendance each morning
Lunch/drink monitor	retrieves lunch boxes from lunchroom

 To simplify classroom organization, choose five to six jobs to assign to students. Some jobs can be a combination of tasks. For example, the inspector, librarian, or attendance taker can also be assigned to pick up the lunch boxes from the lunch room each day. Having a small number of jobs makes it easier to monitor the monitors. Selecting students to do various classroom jobs can be done in a variety of ways.

Post a "Helpers' Chart." The chart can have pictures illustrating each job, or it can have the name of the job, or both. Use job names that indicate what the job involves. For example, paper passer, color guard, or line leader. Helpers can be chosen weekly or daily depending on your particular class needs. If done weekly, choose helpers first thing Monday morning so they can begin their jobs right away. Daily helpers should be selected early in the morning or even the day before. Be sure students are clear about what each job involves. Student helpers from the week before can assist the new helpers if necessary.

 One way of selecting student helpers is to have each student make a "helping hand" by tracing the outline of a hand onto a piece of construction paper and writing his or her name in the center. Decorate as desired and laminate for durability. Store the hands in a box or envelope labeled "Future Helpers." Each week, choose your helpers' hands and write the corresponding names on the chart. At the end of the week, move the hands to a box labeled "Past Helpers," and choose again. Keep a master record of student helpers and their jobs, disbursing tasks equitably.

 Another way to choose helpers is to write each student's name on a clothespin. Choose one clothespin for each weekly job. Write the helpers that have been selected on the chart for the week.

 Students can also be assigned a number. Write the numbers on a piece of paper or a plastic bottle cap. Place the numbers in a bowl or box. Select numbers to choose student helpers. Once a number has been selected, place it in a separate bowl so that all students have a chance to be helpers before you start over again.

Emergency Drills

Most schools do monthly emergency drills. Some schools inform teachers about upcoming drills. Before the first drill make sure you know which exit you're supposed to use and where you're supposed to take your students. Rehearse the drill prior to the first schoolwide practice evacuation.

 Early in the school year, clearly explain the rules and expectations for student behavior in an emergency situation such as a fire drill, earthquake drill, or other required evacuation. Students must walk in an orderly way out of the building according to your directions.

 Verify district policy regarding removal of personal items during emergency drills. If it's cold outside, and not against district policy, have students grab their coats from the backs of their chairs. Students should walk in single file with their hands to themselves unless you have instructed them otherwise. Require that students be attentive and quiet from the time you line up to leave the building until you re-enter the building after clearance. This "quiet" is important so that students can hear directions and instructions during the drill.

 Show your students where the fire alarms in the building are located and explain how they work. Be sure your students know that pulling a fire alarm when there is not a fire or a suspected fire is against the law.

 The emergency bell may be extremely loud and startle you and your students. Discuss the volume of the signal to prepare them for the loud noise. Encourage students to share stories about fire alarms or other loud noises to quell possible fear. The alarm and drill experience may frighten young children. Be sensitive to their fears and try to calm them.

 Many schools have different types of drills, depending on their location. Be sure to know the types of drills your school has and the corresponding signal. All drills should be treated as if they were a real emergency. Each drill, whether fire, tornado, or earthquake, should be planned for and practiced. Reassure students that, most likely, the drill is a practice, while continuing to require emergency behavior.

 As students exit the room, quickly lead them to the prearranged line-up area. Be sure to visually check your line as you're walking out of the building to be sure everyone is following promptly. Once you get to your designated evacuation spot, immediately conduct a student count.

 Keep a class list with names and phone numbers of all of your students, along with an evacuation map, near the door through which you'll exit. Grab the list on your way out the door. Include the following checklist or create one pertinent to your classroom:

- windows closed?
- lights off?
- student coats?
- emergency kits?
- doors closed?

 Depending on the age of your students, consider assigning a certain student the job of closing the doors and windows and turning off lights before leaving the room. If you have numerous windows and doors, you might want to assign the job to a team of students. If your students aren't old enough to close windows and doors, you will have to do this yourself before leaving the room. Note: It's a good policy to keep windows and doors closed, unless it is absolutely necessary to have them open. In many areas, it is against the fire code to have doors open. Ask your school office about specific regulations.

 Many schools provide each teacher with an emergency tub or bucket. These buckets usually contain bandages, first-aid supplies, large garbage bags, several emergency space blankets, moist towelettes, a pair of scissors, masking tape, toilet paper, plastic bags, and some hard candies. If your school does not provide a classroom kit, ask your parent group to provide supplies or funding for you to make your own. If you have to make your own kit, use a plastic bucket with a lid and handle to hold enough provisions for a two-day period. Remember, you have to carry the bucket, so don't make it too heavy.

More and more schools require that parents provide individual emergency kits for their children. These kits generally contain provisions for a two-day period. Kit items include: a space blanket, a flashlight with two batteries, a large garbage bag, two pop-top cans of tuna, two individual serving boxes of cereal, three granola bars, two candy bars, three juice boxes, two individual servings of fruit in a can, a spoon, a letter of encouragement from home, a family photo, emergency contacts, and medical information. All items can be stored in a large resealable bag clearly labeled with the student's name. Store individual bags in a large plastic garbage can with wheels. If possible, store the can outside your classroom during school hours for easy access in the event of an emergency.

 Discuss fire drills and their purpose with your students. Explain that in case there's ever a real emergency, it's important to practice how to leave the building in an orderly fashion. Encourage students to share their ideas, providing ample time for questions.

 After each fire drill, debrief with students. Compliment them on their appropriate behaviors and remind them if improvement is necessary. Give them time to discuss their reactions and feelings to the drill.

 If possible and appropriate for your grade level, invite firefighters to visit the classroom. This gives students an opportunity to see firefighters close up and to ask questions. A field trip to a fire station can also be productive.

Assemblies

Many schools have school-wide assemblies throughout the year. Most assemblies are held in the campus' largest room, which may be a gym or cafeteria. Students are generally required to sit on the floor during an assembly. Explain your expectations and rules for assembly behavior before attending your first campus gathering. Assembly behavior should begin as soon as you leave your classroom and continue until the assembly is over and you've returned back to class. Students should be respectful and polite. Additional rules may vary depending on your school's requirements. If possible, explain in advance what the assembly is about. This will help students be more active listeners. Pose several questions for them to consider during the program. Discuss the answers when you return to class.

 Listen attentively and monitor your students during the program. If it's necessary to discipline a child during the assembly, do it discreetly. Tell students ahead of time what motions or facial expressions you will use to give them information during the assembly. Some examples of useful facial expressions are: a frown to discourage talking, hands on ears to encourage listening, and folded arms to remind students to keep their hands to themselves.

Bathroom Use

Your students will undoubtedly need to go to the bathroom during the day. Recess and break times are good opportunities for this, but students are usually engaged in playing and do not see this as prime bathroom time. Decide how you will handle the bathroom issue in your classroom so that it is the least distracting.

 One method is to use hall or bathroom passes to regulate the number of students leaving the classroom at the same time. A hall or bathroom pass also gives students permission to be out of the room without a teacher. Most teachers choose to place the passes near the door where students can access them without disrupting the class. Bathroom passes should be large enough so they will not be easily lost, soft enough so they won't hurt a child, and "noiseless" enough to not be distracting. A variety of objects can be used—a tennis ball attached to a string, a plastic baby toy, or a cardboard square. As you are picking your objects, keep in mind that you will probably need to replace passes throughout the year.

 Having students carry a bathroom pass to the bathroom with them exposes the pass to all kinds of germs. To avoid this exposure, have a student place the bathroom pass on his or her desk while in the bathroom. This lets the teacher know where the student is, and the pass stays clean.

 If you choose not to use passes, be sure to have some way for students to inform you that they are leaving the room. A hand signal can be used. This way a student can inform you that he or she has to go to the bathroom without distracting the class.

 Another method is to have clothespins with each student's name on it stored near the door in a small container. Have a large tagboard "B" attached to the wall near the door. Leave the edges of the "B" unattached so clothespins can be clipped to the edge as a student leaves for the bathroom. The container holding the clothespins should be user friendly so it is easy to find names, as some students do not have a lot of extra time on the way to the bathroom. (Avoid using clothespins for too many different purposes, as this may be confusing to your students. Use clothespins for no more than one or two purposes, and choose alternative systems for the others.)

Another signal is having a student place a colored index card on his or her desk before leaving the room. This informs you that the student is in the bathroom. When he or she comes back from the bathroom, the card is removed by the student and replaced in the storage area. These cards can be stored in an envelope, or on the chalkboard ledge.

 Encourage students to wash their hands after they go to the bathroom, demonstrating proper procedure. Hands should also be washed before they eat snacks or lunch. By having parents provide containers of moist towelettes you can avoid long lines at the sink. Towelettes can be pooled for class use. Store them near the sink and pass them out to students before snack or lunch. They're also handy to use on inevitable clothing stains.

 If a student's bathroom use is excessive, talk to his or her parent or guardian. The child may have an undetected medical condition, or a reaction to stress.

If you have young students, keep a collection of spare clothes. These can be obtained from a local thrift store or parent donations. Have a range of sizes for both boys and girls. Allow students to borrow the clothes as necessary, placing their soiled clothes in a sealable plastic bag and sent home for parents to wash and return to school. Establish a zero tolerance policy for teasing of any kind, including bathroom accidents.

Daily Schedules

Daily schedules provide an overview of what the day holds. Schedules can be written directly on the board or they can be written on reusable cards. These cards can be made from sentence strips or tagboard. Write one daily activity on each card and then laminate the cards. They can then be placed in a store-bought sentence strip holder or taped directly to the board. A daily schedule might include the following such as the list on the right:

WHAT'S UP?
Today's Happenings

✓ Journal
✓ Math
✓ Snack
✓ Sharing
✓ * (symbol for recess)
✓ Spelling
✓ ** (lunch and recess)
✓ Reading groups
✓ Library
✓ Music
✓ Group work
✓ Cleanup
✓ Dismissal

 Students like to know what their day will include. Post the day's schedule somewhere in the room. Use a heading for the schedule that reflects its importance. Options might include: "Our Daily Work," "Important News," "Priorities," "Now" (for work you will do today), and "Later" (for work that is coming up). If the daily schedule changes, be sure to inform students.

 If your students are too young to read independently, use pictures, along with the words, to illustrate the schedule.

 Even if your students do not appear to be referring to the schedule, continue to post it. In time, they'll come to rely upon it.

 Daily schedules can include the times activities will occur. There are both pros and cons for using times. For very young students, times may be distracting, while older students (second grade and older) may find them useful. Using time limits flexibility since students will keep track of the clock.

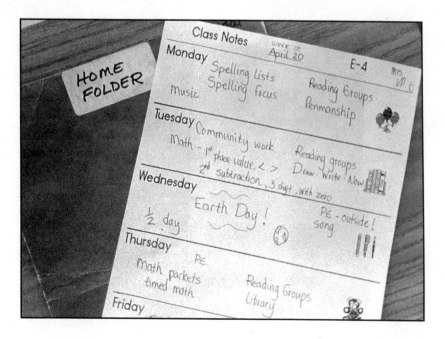

A daily schedule can also be more casual and include only highlights of the day. Using words like *now* and *later* or abbreviations like *a.m.* and *p.m.* can give your schedule a more general nature such as:

a.m.	p.m.
math, reading, spelling, snack	science, penmanship, music, computer

Use symbols for repetitive events like recess. An asterisk (*) can be used to represent short recesses, and two asterisks (**) can be used for longer recesses.

Field Trips

Field trips can be fabulous experiences for your students, but keeping forms and paperwork organized can be a challenge for the teacher. Keep in mind that you want things to go as smoothly as possible for everyone involved. This includes students, parents, bus drivers, school secretaries, business office secretaries, merchants, and anyone else involved in the field trip.

 As you plan the trip, create a file folder of all the papers you accumulate. Write significant phone numbers on the front of the folder for easy access.

 Use a large manila envelope to collect student permission slips and field-trip money. Write the name of each student who turns in a permission slip on the front of the envelope before placing the permission slip inside. If a student also brings in money for the trip, write a dollar symbol next to his or her name on the front of the envelope.

 If volunteers are needed for the field trip, be sure to ask for parent helpers when you send home the field-trip announcement. Many parents and guardians work and will need to request time off, so send notes home well in advance of the trip.

 If a student's parent volunteers to go on the field trip, mark a "V" next to his or her name on the front of the envelope. This will give you a quick view of how many parents you're expecting. If parents are required to pay a fee, place an additional dollar symbol next to the student's name and check it off once the parent has paid.

Be sure parents understand that it will be necessary for them to supervise not only their children, but other children as well. Each volunteer should be given a list of students they will supervise. An index card

works well for this list. Keep a master list of parent/student matches.

 If you are traveling a long distance, you may want to prepare lap boards for each student. Lap boards can be made by collecting math papers, puzzles, hidden pictures, scrambled sentences, and a variety of other worksheets that fit your students' ability level. Attach the papers inside a file folder by placing two or three staples at the top of the opened folder. Punch a hole in the folder and attach a pencil with a string. Make a pencil holder by cutting two ½" (1.25 cm) slits, 4" (10.2 cm) apart, in the top inside section of the folder in the style of a clipboard. Slip the pencil into the cutout sleeve. The file folder will provide a hard surface on which students can write, and will keep their pencil handy.

 Be sure to carry some extra items with you on your field trip. A field trip checklist might include:

- extra pencils with erasers
- extra lap boards
- bandages
- list of parent helpers and students
- copy of permission slips
- name, address, and phone number of person at destination
- name, address, and phone number of person at school site
- first-aid kit

Respond promptly to a parent or guardian's offer to help. Communicate your needs by sending home the following confirmation letter on page 30:

Field Trip Volunteer Form

Dear Parent or Guardian,

Thank you for volunteering to accompany us on our field trip to

_____ on _____.

_____ We have plenty of helpers for this trip.

_____ May we call you if we have cancellations?
How much advance notice do you need?

_____

_____ Yes, we could use your help supervising a group of students.

Please arrive at the school at _____(a.m. p.m.)
so we can go over details of the trip.

_____ The fee for chaperons for this trip is _____ .

_____ There is no fee for chaperons for this trip.

Your support is greatly appreciated!

Sincerely,

_____

© Fearon Teacher Aids FE7972

Classroom Management

In managing a classroom, your goal should be to create a safe environment for children and adults. Find a management style that works for you and reflects caring, sincerity, and respect. The most important word in classroom management is *respect*. Without it, you and your students cannot create a positive learning environment. Model it, teach it, nurture it, give it, and receive it.

 Establish your expectations for classroom behavior beginning on the first day of school. Your expectations should include the use of good manners, a demonstration of courtesy, kindness, and tolerance.

Post classroom rules. Review and discuss classroom standards so that everyone knows what is expected. Rules might include information about bringing pencils, not chewing gum, and not running in the halls. Expectations for learning, such as the following, should also be included:

- *Be considerate of others*
- *Share your best self*
- *Be responsible for your own learning*
- *If you need help—ask!*

 Many schools have standardized discipline policies. Be familiar with your school and district's specific policies. If your school does not have a standard policy, check with other teachers at your grade level to see what they they do. Find a plan that you believe in and can enforce without hesitation.

Once you've decided on a discipline plan, explain it to your students and parents. Be sure that you are clear and precise so that your expectations are understood. If you send home a written discipline policy, request that parents return a form that states they've read and understood the material.

A multistep discipline plan allows students to change their behavior along the way and avoid negative consequences. An example of a multistep plan might take the following form:

Step One:
Verbal warning about behavior

Step Two:
Name is written on the board

Step Three:
Check by name

Step Four:
Loss of privileges (recess, free time)

 If the student changes the behavior after Step Two, erase his or her name from the board. If the behavior changes after Step Three, erase the check. If the student does not change his or her behavior after Step Four, it's time to phone home to explain the situation to a parent or guardian.

You may have some students who need constant reinforcement regarding their behavior. It may be necessary to develop a contract. A contract can be as simple as an index card taped to the student's desk. Each time an appropriate behavior is noticed, a sticker can be added to the card by the teacher. The student's goal is to earn a certain number of stickers to win a privilege such as, lunchtime with the teacher, extra free time, or a special activity. Send the card home at the end of the week for parents to review. Each week, start a new card.

For a simple management system, an "Oops Board" can be effective. When students forget what they should be doing, forget their manners, or forget how to be considerate of others, list their names on the board. Prior to putting their names on the board, give them fair warning.

- Once on the board, if a student changes his or her behavior, erase the name with no further consequences.

- If behavior doesn't change before recess or free time, he or she must forfeit a play time. Be sure to report this to parents, either by a quick phone call or a note home. Purchase a stamp with the word *Oops* on it and use it to stamp the student's daily calendar. This lets parents know that the student has lost a privilege because of unacceptable behavior.

Teaching students about feelings and how to handle them is an important aspect of a classroom management plan. Be sure your students know that it is all right to have feelings. We all feel angry, happy, sad, mad, tired, frustrated, excited, and so on. Students need to learn to manage those feelings. Consider posting the following thought-provoking reminder in your room:

It's OK to be mad.
It's not OK to be mean.

Provide your students with a list of the following problem-solving options:

- Give an "I" message (a message starting with the word *I*)
- Walk away
- Talk it over
- Ignore the behavior
- Do something else
- Ask for help

Encourage students to interact as a school family. Remind them that they will be spending a lot of time together. They have the opportunity to create an inspiring, productive, and significant relationship with their school family.

Provide students with an opportunity to discuss problems and concerns they have regarding behaviors. Keep a Worry Bee in your classroom. A Worry Bee can be made out of yellow and black construction paper and then laminated. Attach a magnet to the back so students can hang the Worry Bee on the board when they have a concern or worry. The Worry Bee is your cue to take time to hear a student's worry and discuss the problem as a class. To avoid tattling, inform students that they must have tried two problem-solving options before posting the Worry Bee.

CHAPTER THREE

Organizing Math

Math is taught in a number of ways, depending on which strategy your school district has adopted. While the textbooks and order in which math principles are taught vary, the importance of math is the same in every school. Your goal is to teach students to love math. Teach them to embrace it as a science that has guided, frustrated, and fascinated humankind since ancient times. Whatever early math experiences you may have had, teach your students that math is a fascinating tool.

Manipulatives

Manipulatives are objects that can be held, moved, and manipulated by your students. They are especially important for kinesthetic learners who need to experience things through touch and movement in order to understand. Manipulatives are also an important tool for demonstrating abstract concepts in a real and tangible way. For a lot of students, manipulatives can be the bridge that makes math a topic they can relate to themselves.

 Be creative when choosing manipulatives. Try beans, plastic animals of any kind, plastic chips, plastic cubes, straws, or small erasers. Don't use anything that will rot, break, or wear out easily.

 Before introducing a new manipulative, give students an opportunity to explore and play with it. This will allow students to focus on the math problem—not the manipulative—when you're ready to use them for math calculations.

 Try to offer several types of manipulatives. This will allow you to rotate them periodically so they won't lose their appeal. Students will be more apt to pick up a manipulative if it looks new and interesting. As you rotate them, keep the ones you're not using out of sight. Then, when they do come out again, they'll seem new.

 To foster independence, store manipulatives in an easily—accessible spot.

 Make manipulatives an accepted part of your math class rather than just an occasional prop. This will help students see manipulatives as a viable resource and not a crutch.

 Keep small containers, such as portion cups, jar lids, or small paper cups nearby the manipulatives for students to carry back manipulatives to their desks. Using small containers encourages students to take only what they need.

 Occasionally wash the manipulatives in hot, soapy water to avoid bacteria growth.

 When collecting manipulatives, think about how they will contribute to classroom noise level. Noisy manipulatives can distract other students while they are working.

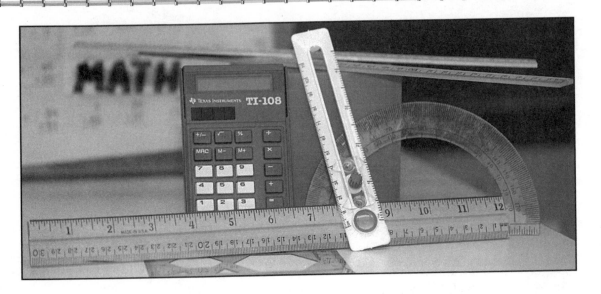

 Have a variety of math tools—slide rule, protractor, compass, T-square, calculator, abacus—on hand for students to explore. This helps them see the flexibility of math. Explain each tool's use to whatever degree satisfies students' curiosity. The explanation need not be all-encompassing. Encourage students to use them in their own inventive ways.

 Discard any broken, chipped, or peeling manipulatives to ensure safety. Maintaining high standards will reinforce students' belief that math is important and respected.

Content

The content of your math curriculum is often spelled out for you in the table of contents of the math book or in the district curriculum guide. This can be valuable information and an excellent list of topics to cover. However, it's always wise to present topics in a sequence that makes sense to you, regardless of textbook suggestions. If you don't understand the suggested sequence, it's unlikely that your students will either.

 Vary the intensity of the math topics by presenting a short topic after a long and involved one.

 Explain to your students the relationship between the chapter you're currently working on, the chapter you've just finished, and the next chapter. This helps them get the "big picture" of what they are learning and how it all fits together.

 Make problems relevant to the class whenever possible. An example of Billy who watched five hours of TV on Tuesday and two hours on Wednesday, will be much clearer than the example of Mr. Bond who lost five points on the stock market on Tuesday and two points on Wednesday.

 If students don't understand a particular concept, do not move on, even if the math book does. Be sure students understand the material. Let your students guide you in determining how much time to spend on a topic rather than adhering rigidly to the number of pages or problems the math book allots.

 Whenever possible, let your students see, hear, and experience the concepts they are learning. This will raise their retention and comprehension rate.

Use accurate mathematical terminology even for very young students. Never use silly words for math operations or concepts. Using correct mathematical language from the beginning means that students won't have to waste time unlearning and relearning new language later on. Present your students with the opportunity to use the correct words for mathematical processes and they will happily rise to the occasion.

 Make math fun. This may be something that no one ever did for you, but it is a great gift you can pass on to your students. Use chocolate chips, raisins, plastic flies, or M&Ms™ for counting, adding, subtracting, multiplying, dividing, ratios, fractions, estimation, probability, and anything else you can think of. When using edible manipulatives, pass out individual quantities to each child on a clean paper towel, and when the lesson is over, the manipulatives may be eaten. Don't allow students to swap edible manipulatives.

Incorporate as many learning styles into your math lessons as possible. Let students sing, dance, draw, talk, ponder, and write about math. This will increase understanding and make math fun at the same time.

 Teach your students that there are often many ways to arrive at an answer. Allow students to share their brain processes with the class. This will help your students see that one answer can be arrived at through a variety of methods. It will also help you see how your students are processing. This information will be helpful when a redirection in the thought process is needed.

Products

The products from your math lessons will be mainly papers full of math calculations. Your students will do math pages, operation worksheets, math tests, problem-solving worksheets, story problems and lots more. Try to vary your products in small ways whenever you can. Offer a variety of materials—from construction to graph paper—on which to work out problems. For a change, have students use crayons or paint for calculations.

 Allow students to display their math work. Use a special bulletin board to display work or create a class book that can be updated periodically. A class book can be made by labeling a binder "I Am Proud of My Math," and providing plastic page protectors. Label each page protector with a student's name so each child can place "proud math work" in his or her own page protector. Have the binder accessible so students can add work and view others' accomplishments.

 On large drawing paper, have students illustrate, without using any words, how they did a math problem.

 Have students write about how they solved a math problem. See if another student can follow the procedure and get the same results.

 Allow the use of calculators. This is a valuable skill for students to learn, and they enjoy the change.

Evaluation

As you guide students though the math curriculum, you'll want to be able to determine their progress. There are many forms of evaluation. Some are informal and can be done quickly. Others are more formal and take more time to prepare, administer, and correct. Before committing to a particular form of evaluation, ask yourself if it accurately measures the skills you deem important.

There are many purposes in evaluating student work. The purpose of your evaluation may be to answer one or more of the following questions:

Are students participating?

Are students getting the correct answers?

Do students understand the steps to take to get an answer?

Do students understand the general concept being taught?

Do students see how the concept fits into a large picture?

Can students complete the process quickly?

Can students explain how they did the process?

 Once you decide your purpose, choose a method of evaluation that best provides the information you're seeking.

 Evaluate students by asking them to hold up their answers on their fingers, slates, or individual papers.

 Help students to evaluate themselves by asking them to compare answers with a classmate.

 Have students raise their hands when they think they know an answer. Walk around and let students whisper their answers in your ear. Let them know if their answers are right or wrong.

 Check student work by walking around and looking over their shoulders as they work.

 Have a student work a problem on the board so you can see his or her understanding of the process. Ask classmates if they agree. Be sure to foster an atmosphere of helpfulness and not criticism.

 Have students describe, in writing, how they arrived at an answer.

 Have students draw a picture describing their process.

 Give a pop quiz. Such unannounced tests are short in length and cover recent skills. The quiz can be given orally, written on the board, passed out to each student.

 Hand out a worksheet with completed math problems. Make sure some problems are incorrect. Have students identify correct and incorrect answers.

 Depending on the age of your students, use formal tests. These tests generally have 20–50 problems and cover a variety of skills. Before giving the test, decide if you will allow students to ask questions once the test has begun.

 Prior to the test, tell students what they'll be expected to know. Give them plenty of time to study.

 Always provide feedback on tests. This can be done in a group session, in which students are allowed to ask questions about problems they missed.

CHAPTER FOUR

Organizing Reading

Content Ideas

Excellence in reading involves a whole spectrum of skills your students must learn. Basic skills include recognizing letters and words, understanding phonic rules, and sounding out unfamiliar words. More complex skills include silent reading with comprehension, making evaluations and inferences from what was read, and fluency in reading aloud. No matter how old your students are, address all skills throughout the year. Older students will focus more on advanced skills, but will benefit from a review of basic skills. Younger students will enjoy dabbling in more advanced skills on an introductory level.

Reading is a skill that is important in many aspects of daily life. People of all ages use reading for accessing information, following instructions, entertainment, communicating emotions and information, and general survival purposes. The content of your reading program should make students aware of the many purposes of reading.

Your reading program should include many different topics, genres, and cultural influences. Exposure to many writing styles, individual perspectives, and opinions will enhance students' reading experiences.

A well-rounded reading program should also provide students with the opportunity to complete a task by following written directions. Students can read for directions in a variety of situations. Some examples include board-game instructions, worksheet directions, and steps in completing a process.

Communication is an essential part of a successful and well-rounded reading program. Students should have opportunities to talk about what they read. A good way to do this is to assign projects that require individual products that can be made in a small-group setting. The process is like a group of very young children engaged in parallel play; they are near each other but do not actually merge their play. As students work together, the topic of discussion should be open and flexible. This kind of a group setting allows students to communicate in a safe and regulated environment.

Reading sets the foundation upon which all other learning is built. In your classroom, whatever the grade level, reading must be taught, modeled, and discussed daily. To be successful, your students not only need the skills to read, but also the desire to read. It is your attitude toward reading that will set the stage for your students' reading success. No matter which reading program your school or district requires you to use, it is up to you to give your students a taste for the richness that awaits them through reading. Passing on to your students a passion for reading will be one of your greatest achievements.

 Your reading program should give students opportunities to practice how to gather information from newspapers, encyclopedias, dictionaries, and nonfiction books of all kinds. After researching a particular topic, it's important to provide students with ways to share knowledge. Encourage them to create posters, draw pictures, design time lines, or prepare outlines or reports.

 Store teacher's editions close to your desk. Keep an index card in each book to mark where the group finished reading. On the index card, write the date and the last page that was read. This makes it easy for parent helpers to pick up the book and know exactly where the group should be reading.

 Books used for reading groups should be stored on a shelf or in an accessible spot where students can reach them. Store each group's books together. Encourage students to be responsible for retrieving and returning books.

 Decide how many days of the week reading will be conducted in groups and as a whole class. Your schedule can be structured in a variety of ways and will reflect your own classroom needs. Generally, you'll want to have students meet in small groups at least three days a week. Each time the group meets they'll do a different activity. For example, on Day 1, the group may read aloud to an adult in a round-robin style. On Day 2, they may work on a workbook assignment. Day 3 may find them working together on individual projects in a small-group setting.

 On the days the class meets as a whole, a variety of reading activities can be done. Discuss story elements, including plot, setting, character development, conflict, and resolution. Other activities might include choral reading, play production, book report presentations, and reading book reviews in newspapers.

Reading Groups

Reading lessons can be presented to the class as a whole or in small groups. If you have several reading levels, arrange groups by ability. Decide on a manageable number of groups for your classroom, as each group must be led by the teacher or other qualified adult. Depending on class size, you may end up with three or four groups.

 Allow students to select names for their reading groups. Ahead of time, discuss the decision-making process so students will know how to proceed. Remind them that since one name is to be chosen, everyone must work together to pick a name.

 Invite parent helpers to be reading-group leaders. Recruit them to work with a group of students each week on a particular day at a particular time. Each time a new helper starts, offer guidelines as to what's expected of them and how much direction they should give students. Urge parents to inform you if they're unable to come on their scheduled day so you can arrange a backup plan.

Each student should experience group reading in a small-group setting a minimum of twice a week. If you have enough parent helpers to do this, have students work on spelling and workbook assignments. This will provide extra time for a second small group. A schedule, which includes two small-group sessions per week, could be structured like this:

DAYS	GROUP 1	GROUP 2	GROUP 3	GROUP 4
MONDAY	group	group	spelling/workbook	project
TUESDAY	spelling/workbook	group	project	group
THURSDAY	group	project	group	spelling/workbook
FRIDAY	project	spelling/workbook	group	group

As groups talk about a book they've read, ask:

What made the characters likable, believable, or heroic?

What was your favorite part, and why?

Why did the author write the book?

How would you change the book if you wrote it?

Did the pictures in the book fit the story? Why or why not?

Did you like the way the book ended?

Would you recommend the book? To whom would you recommend it, and why?

Keep a chart showing what each reading group will be doing during the week. Post the schedule for students to review.

Teach students to work independently. This will free you to work with a small group while other students work on their own. Training students to work independently takes time and is a difficult skill for some children to master. To ensure success, match the task to the student's ability level. Tasks that are too difficult will discourage independence.

Independent work situations are best used for reviewing skills that have already been presented, rather than introducing new ones. Be sure that all instructions are presented clearly. A good way to check student understanding is by having various students repeat the instructions out loud.

© Fearon Teacher Aids FE7972

Materials

A classroom should have both traditional and non-traditional reading material in order to encourage well-rounded reading. In addition to textbooks, basic readers, and library books, provide a wide variety of materials for students to read, including comic books, magazines, maps, atlases, and baseball cards.

 Create a cozy reading nook using a large appliance box. Maneuver the box so that the open end faces the ceiling, allowing enough light for reading. Cut out a side section for easy access. Place it against a wall for stability and line with pillows or rug squares.

 Students are more likely to abide by reading-room rules if they help write them. Encourage them to determine what the standards will be.

 A great way to reinforce reading skills is by offering students books on tape. Send home blank audiotapes on which parents can record stories. In addition to increasing your audio library, this involves parents in the educational process.

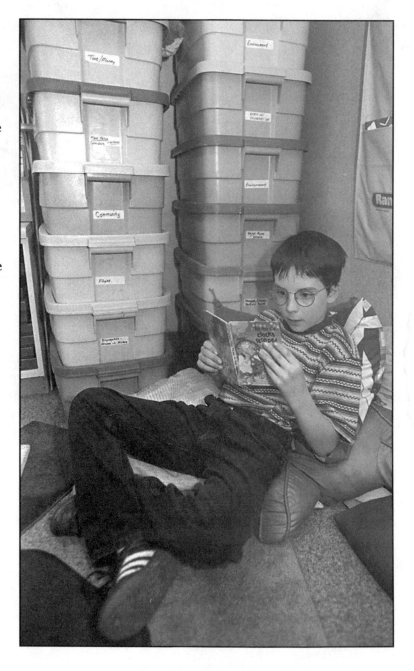

 Offer books which reflect a wide range of reading levels. Provide books on many different subjects, and allow students to suggest topics for new books. Take advantage of new interests as they arise. Your school librarian will be an invaluable asset in choosing suitable books. Sometimes an unexpected diversion can create fascinating results.

 Even if your students aren't yet reading, expose them to reference books of all kinds.

 Provide two to four copies of certain books in your classroom to encourage group reading. Groups can then discuss the book—whether or not they liked it, and why.

CHAPTER FIVE

Organizing Language Arts and Spelling

At one time educators believed that rote and routine were the most important aspects of language arts and spelling. Dissection and deciphering words were more important than creative composition. Over the last several years, however, the emphasis has fortunately broadened. Teachers now expose students to the limitless possibilities of language. In your classroom, use these subjects as springboards to imagination and creativity.

Language arts covers the use and organization of language and is prominently displayed throughout the classroom. In all of your student interactions, you convey the message that language is an invaluable tool to be studied and understood.

Language Arts Ideas

Language arts covers a broad spectrum of topics, including identifying parts of speech, using proper grammar, formatting written communication, and identifying contextual meanings. Language arts is a subject amenable to as much flexibility as you care to build into it. Making a long-term plan will help you blend in all the subject's various facets at suitable times.

It's best to teach English basics and its usage in a logical order, beginning with nouns and then verbs. Once students are familiar with nouns and verbs, they're ready to move on to basic sentence structure. When students are able to write an individual sentence, they're ready to learn about writing paragraphs, letters, stories, and reports.

When teaching the basics be sure to include:

Nouns—common and proper (subject)

Verbs—being and action (predicate)

Adjectives—describing words

Adverbs—expressing time, place, or degree

Sentence Requirements—capitalization, subject, predicate, punctuation

Quotations—punctuation, correct usage

Sentence Questions—question, statement, exclamation, command

Paragraph Formation—opening sentence, body, closing sentence

Letters—heading, salutation, body, closing, signature

Stories—beginning, middle, end

Research—problem statement, hypothesis, research, conclusion

Use your chalkboard/whiteboard to demonstrate correct punctuation, verb tense, sentence structure, and capitalization. Write one or two sentences on the board daily to be copied and discussed. Sentences can be done as a warm-up activity first thing in the morning or as students come in from recess. Sentences can be written correctly and discussed, or students can correct sentences that has been written incorrectly. Have students write sentences correctly in a writing notebook or journal. Include skills in your sentences that you are currently working on. You can focus on just one skill or incorporate many skills in one sentence.

 If you are discussing quotation marks, your sentence could read:

> The cat is acting very strange today said Teresa.

 If you are studying capitalization your sentence might read:

> tim and frank are going to washington, d.c., in august.

 If students are learning about verb tense, write:

> I eated two pizzas I buyed at the store.

 To incorporate many skills, include a variety of mistakes:

> richard goed two school while he were in arizona said tom

 When you are studying sentence types, give students the opportunity to convert a statement to a question, exclamation, or command:

> I cannot go to the store today.
>
> Can I go to the store today?
>
> Oh, no, I can't go to the store!
>
> You go to the store.

 Cut out large, colorful punctuation marks such as a period, question mark, and exclamation point, to place on wall or bulletin board. These can be left up throughout the year for students reference.

 Nouns should be introduced at a very young age. Even students who are not reading can identify nouns around the classroom. Both proper and common nouns should be taught. Once students are able to recognize proper nouns, capitalization will make more sense to them since proper nouns are always capitalized.

 Teaching students about nouns need not be tedious. Games like, "Noun Search" transforms textbook subjects into three-dimensional fun. The object is for students to walk around the room searching for nouns. On the count of three, students stop next to a noun and tell the class its name.

 "Stand-up Nouns" is another game that requires students to stand up every time they hear the teacher say a noun. Another game, "Tell Me a Noun," is used at dismissal time. When you call a student's name for dismissal, have him or her say a noun.

 When studying verbs include both action and being verbs. Action verbs are those that show action; they are fun and easy to act out. Your study of being verbs can be limited to the five most commonly used—*is, was, am, are,* and *were.*

 Once students understand nouns and verbs, show them how they're used in a sentence. Every sentence has four requirements—a capital at the beginning, punctuation at the end, and a noun and verb in between. Once students learn these elements they will be able to write and recognize sentences.

When the basic elements of a sentence are understood, other word accessories can be added. These accessories can include adjectives, adverbs, complex subjects, and predicates and prepositional phrases. The age of your students and your long-term goal will help you decide which elements need to be taught and in what sequence.

As students learn to write sentences, teach them about the different types of sentences. Help students recognize the difference between a statement, a question, a command, and an exclamation. Demonstrate the punctuation used in each type of sentence.

After they've mastered writing individual sentences, have students progress to writing a paragraph. Teach children about the different purposes and kinds of paragraphs. Show them paragraphs that give directions, offer an opinion, tell a story, and try to convince. The more exposure students have to different kinds of writing the better writers they will become.

Once students can recognize and identify the basic structure of a sentence, guide them in whatever direction meets your class's specific needs and requirements. No matter what your goal—whether writing sentences or doing research reports—your students need to have a basic foundation before proceeding. Teaching nouns and verbs will be the beginning of that foundation.

Spelling Ideas

Spelling can be presented in a variety of ways. A common teaching tool is the spelling test. Word lists are generally given to students on Monday and students are tested Friday. Depending on your students' age, you may require them to study the words on their own during the week, or you may present lessons focusing on the spelling list throughout the week.

 Students can be given a pretest on Monday to determine which of their spelling words they need to focus on the most. Students who spell all the words correctly on Monday can be given a more difficult list to study for the week, or they can be given an alternative assignment such as using the words to write a paragraph or story.

 Spelling lists can come from a variety of sources. Words that students use and misspell can be used as individual spelling lists. To do this, make a file folder for each student. Each time the student writes a story or assignment, scan his or her work for misspelled words. Write these words in his or her file folder and use them as part of an individualized spelling program. Have parent helpers or older students test students using the lists.

 Words can also be generated from a unit or story the class is currently studying. Choose words related to the topic and provide students with a list of these words to be part of the spelling test. Spelling textbooks are also a good source of spelling lists and will generally include activities and assignments students can do.

 Teaching spelling can serve several different purposes in addition to the basic concept of teaching students how to spell particular words. A spelling lesson may focus on teaching new word patterns, such as words containing *igh* or *stp* or *ae* and the rules that govern them. Other purposes include improving memory skills and expanding students' vocabularies. As the school year progresses, address each skill, keeping in mind the purpose behind each lesson.

 When teaching new word patterns present a variety of words that illustrate the pattern. Be sure to include words with which students are familiar, as well as some new words. It's important to explain not only the rule for the word patterns, but also exceptions to the rule. You may want to include one or two exceptions in the list, or explore the rule-breakers in an extended activity.

 Correct word spelling is a great memory tester. While some students may excel in this area, others may find it difficult. When words are handed out on Monday and tested on Friday, it tests short-term memory. Long-term memory skills are measured when spelling words are retested after three weeks. Both memory skills are important and should be incorporated into your lessons.

 Spelling lessons may revolve around thematic topics such as holidays, historical figures, events, the environment, or community. A different theme can be used each week or a theme could be extended for a month or more. Themes should be well thoughtout and organized in advance of the unit. Sufficient time should be allowed for students to explore the theme and immerse themselves before moving on to a new theme.

When giving spelling lists and tests, provide an opportunity for advancement. Students who have successfully passed one level of difficulty should be allowed to advance to a more difficult list. Lists should cover grade levels one level below and at least three levels above. Assign a different color to each list to de-emphasize competition and focus on each student's personal advancement.

 Bonus words can be added to spelling lists. They should be more difficult and challenging. Give younger students the option of trying the bonus words or omitting them.

CHAPTER SIX

Organizing Student Work

Passing Out and Collecting Student Assignments

 When passing out new student work, place a small number of papers at each table or row. Allow students to distribute papers to their row or table mates, and have the last student hold up any extra papers. This saves you from counting the exact number for each row and gives students a chance to be involved in the process. Require students to hold up extras quickly and quietly. Students soon catch on to this time-saving routine.

 Choosing a student to be table or row organizer for a day or week is a good way to have a readily-available helper. Allow the organizer to be responsible for passing out papers to each row or table. Organizers should be changed often, offering every child an opportunity to help. Assignments students do every day should be placed in an easily accessible spot to encourage them to take responsibility for picking them up and completing them. Examples might include a daily activity that is completed every morning upon arrival, or an assignment that is completed each day after recess. Keep the spot the same so students will always know where to find the material.

 Keep a container or basket in your classroom labeled, "Homeward Bound" in which you can place school notices that go home with students. As soon as these items are brought to your mailbox or classroom, place them in the basket. Check the basket before the end of each day so that information can be sent home.

Throughout the year you will handle hundreds of pieces of paper. Most will be student work that eventually ends up in the teacher's file, parent's file, or on the student's desk. Ideally, papers of value should not end up in students' desks, as they are unlikely to emerge again. Keeping track of student work is an organizational challenge. To stay on top of it, you'll need to keep track of which work has been given out and to whom, which work has come in and from whom, and what level of mastery each student has achieved on each piece of work. By using efficient organizational strategies, you'll be able to meet these goals and manage the abundance of student work year after year.

When collecting student work to be corrected, use a colored, plastic, rectangular basket. Keep the basket in front of the room and have students place their finished work in the basket. Always refer to the basket by the same name such as "The Blue Basket." This helps students remember where to stack completed assignments.

You can create separate collection areas for different subjects, such as "Math in," "Spelling in," "Writing in." Clearly labeled dish-washing tubs make useful storage bins. If someone other than you, such as an aide or volunteer, corrects student work, write out specific directions for correcting. Laminate and store in the tub.

 Have a "Ketchup Basket" for not-yet-completed student work. Encourage students to retrieve work and finish, as time permits. Decorate the basket with a real plastic ketchup bottle or pictures of ketchup bottles.

 Consider collecting and displaying student work using a clothesline and clothespins. Use a marker to color the long, flat side of enough clothespins to have one for each student. As students turn in work, use colored clothespins to hang it. If more than one clothespin is needed for a particular piece, use one colored pin and one plain. A quick glance at the clothesline and the unused supply of colored pins will tell you how many students have not turned in their work.

To create a more formal clothesline system, assign students numbers and print them on the flat side of the clothes-pins. Have students write their numbers near their names. Again, a quick glance at the numbers reveals which students have yet to finish the assignment.

Keep a basket in the classroom labeled "Friday Boxes." All the papers that are completed and corrected during the week can be placed in the basket. On Fridays, distribute papers to students' cubby-holes, slots, or file folders. Papers that have no names should be left in the "Friday Boxes" basket to be claimed later. On Friday, have students take their work home.

To give your class an added opportunity to practice listening skills, tell students that they are going to arrange their papers from the "Friday Boxes" into a specific order. Students should place their pile of papers on one side of their desks, leaving an area clear to start a new pile. Use one student's stacks of papers to demonstrate paper order. Hold up one paper at a time for the class to see. Instruct students to find the corresponding paper, hold it up, then place it in their stacks. Sorting through papers this way gives students a chance to claim any unnamed papers left in the "Friday Boxes." While students are arranging papers, have them check to make sure they don't have another student's paper. Staple each pile and send it home for parents to review.

Work to Be Saved or Shared

Throughout the year you may want to save samples of student work to send home or pass on to next year's teacher to show student progress. This work can be saved in a variety of portfolio systems:

 One way to create a student portfolio is to give each student a large manila envelope labeled with his or her name. Every day allow students to add completed and corrected work they want to save. This "Treasure Envelope" will encourage them to take pride in their work. Send the envelopes home once every two weeks to be shared with parents. After viewing the work, parents and students can decide together which work should remain in the "Treasure Envelope." The envelope is then returned to school. Continue this process throughout the year.

 Another way to create student portfolios is to have student file folders. These files can be stored in a file cabinet or desk drawer. At the end of the year, mount each piece of student work on construction paper and bind the papers together with staples, yarn, or spiral spines. This becomes a memory packet of the year's work for each student to take home.

 Student work can also be collected by using large manila envelopes labeled for each month of the school year. Every month choose one or two assignments per child to place in the envelope, making sure names are on them. At the end of the year, collate student papers, then staple or bind them into a packet ready to take home.

 Students can be included in selecting work that they'd like to have in their portfolios. Collect work throughout the year that represents a variety of skills and mastery. Store these, and at the end of the year have students sort through their work, selecting items they'd like to put into their portfolios. Suggest criteria for saveable items. Students should look for work that represents their progress and effort. Mount or otherwise package material for students to take home. Depending on the age of your students and the needs and requirements of your district, you may need to develop a more complex portfolio system. There are many books, articles, and web sites covering this topic.

To encourage students to share their work and compliment the work of others, keep a box in which students can place work they'd like to share with the class. This work might include drawings, tests, or written assignments. Designate a specific day and time for group sharing. Make positive comments and ask, "How was it done?"

 Create a "Proud Work" binder using plastic page protectors (available at office or variety stores). In the lower left-hand corner of each page protector, write a student's name. Students can then place work in the binder that they would like to share with the class. Invite them to add work each week. Before work goes into the binder, it should be teacher-corrected. Keep the binder in the reading area or another accessible spot. The page protectors can then be sent home at the end of the year with each student.

Giving Feedback on Student Work

Celebrate the work your students do. Let them know that their work is not only important to you, but also to their parents. The more immediate the feedback, the more productive it becomes. Use a variety of methods for complimenting work. Students of all ages enjoy stickers, stamps, and personal notes. Vary your use of these items.

Keep a sticker basket in your classroom. Allow students to place stickers on their completed and corrected work. Determine your criteria for sticker use.

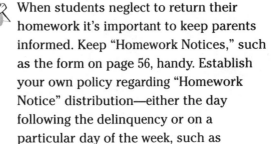

Create a work slip to send home with work that was not completed at school and needs to be done at home. Make a work slip using a half sheet of paper and include the following information: student's name, date, work to be completed, and date to be returned. Keep blank forms on hand.

Explain to students that a work slip does not mean the student is being punished or penalized. Work slips merely provide parents with information regarding what is expected by the teacher.

In order to be sure parents see the work, ask them to sign the papers and have their children return them to school.

Provide some kind of feedback on all student work. Feedback may be as simple as a smiley face indicating that the work has been seen. More detailed feedback may involve a phrase or note written specifically to each student. Adjust your feedback according to the depth and complexity of the assignment, but it is important that children know you have taken the time to look over their work.

When students neglect to return their homework it's important to keep parents informed. Keep "Homework Notices," such as the form on page 56, handy. Establish your own policy regarding "Homework Notice" distribution—either the day following the delinquency or on a particular day of the week, such as every Friday.

Homework Notice

_____
(date)

Dear _____ ,

Your child _____

needs to work on his/her _____

_____

and return it to school by _____ .

Thank you,

_____

     Reproducible

CHAPTER SEVEN

Organizing Communication

The ability to communicate with students, parents, and staff may well be the most critical element in achieving success as a teacher. Effective communication is vital to the creation of positive rapport with colleagues. Communication skills are an essential foundation on which professional success is founded.

In written communication, our message is colored by the words we choose, the clarity of our thoughts, appearance, and neatness, and overall appropriateness.

In oral communication, far more is involved. We send out messages through body posture, hand gestures, eye contact, facial expressions, and voice inflections. It's important to be aware of these influences because they communicate who we are and our attitude about teaching. Successful communication presumes a sincere respect for others, a quality that can't be faked, especially around children.

Sending out positive messages increases your effectiveness as a teacher. Positive messages take many forms and share important feelings of sincerity and caring.

"I am listening and I want to hear what you have to say."

"I am available to hear you when you need to be heard.",

"I think what you have to say is important, and I care about you."

"I like who you are."

Negative messages, on the other hand, can decrease your effectiveness as a teacher and destroy your student's trust in you. Negative messages are sent, not only through our words, but through our actions.

"I am not listening even though I am pretending to."

"I am busy and I do not want to listen to you."

"What I have to say is more important than what you have to say."

"I really don't care."

Effective communication requires an awareness of the many messages we send and how we send them. As a teacher you will have the opportunity to touch your students' lives daily through your sincere and caring communication.

Communicating with Students

Whether consciously or not, you are always communicating with your students, both verbally and non-verbally. Keep your communication positive and caring. As a teacher you play an important role in the life of each of your students. Never make remarks to or around students that might hurt their feelings.

 When you are first learning your students' names, think of a fun word, such as "jellybean" or "lollipop," as a substitute for a temporarily forgotten name. This is much more endearing than saying, "You in the blue shirt."

 Greet each student as he or she arrives in the classroom. Use the child's name in your greeting and show enthusiasm. This helps children feel welcome and valued.

Call students by name as often as possible. Use their names in positive instances—not only when you admonish them.

Teach your class to respect the importance of a person's name. If a student has a nickname they like to be called, always try to use it. Do not allow students to call others by nicknames unless the individual agrees. Don't allow students to alter or shorten a classmate's name without his or her permission.

Children occasionally go through periods of wanting to change their names to something entirely different. Respect their desire, if it's not too distracting to class routine. The desire for a name change sometimes reflects a particular situation the child is experiencing and this is his or her way of processing.

 Remember, your students thrive on connecting with you. Take time to share "small talk," with them. Inquire about their dogs, cats, brothers, or sisters. Mention, to the class, if you see a student at the store, library, or soccer field.

 Have a space on the blackboard or whiteboard where you write positive notes to the class, such as:

"I appreciate your hard work yesterday."

"I am looking forward to seeing your projects this afternoon."

"I feel like the luckiest teacher in the school."

 Write messages on sticky notes to individual students and place them on their desks before they arrive at school. Appropriate notes might include a special thank you for a job well done; recognition of an effort made; a comment about a show-and-tell item; or, simply wishing them a happy day. Keep track of which students you have written to so that no one will be left out or overly favored.

 Keep a pad of decorative paper in your desk to use on birthdays. Have birthday students come to the front of the room and dictate what they want you to write about their birthdays. It may include how old they'll be, what they plan to do to celebrate, how they're looking forward to turning a year older, what special treats they might eat, or what presents they hope to get. Students then take the paper home as a birthday remembrance. Be sensitive to children who may not celebrate birthdays and holidays.

 Keep a supply of picture postcards to use as a special surprise. Two or three times a year, write a positive message to each student and place the card in his or her cubby-holes or mailboxes.

 Keep a box in your classroom labeled "Teacher's Treasures." Keep all drawings, paintings, and paper gifts of love from your students. Storing them in this way helps children feel valued.

Encourage students to write to you. Have a mailbox or cubbyhole where students can place notes and letters to you.

 Your communication is important, not only with your own students, but with all students in the school. Extend your communication beyond your own classroom by talking to students as you go down the hall or walk around the lunchroom. Take time to share a comment or ask a question. Don't let the fact that you do not know their names stop you from talking to them. Many students in your school will certainly know your name even if you don't know theirs. Establishing yourself as generally friendly and approachable cannot help but increase your effectiveness as a communicator and as a teacher.

Communicating with Students' Parents

The first few weeks of school is the time is to set the tone for future communication with parents. Let them know that you welcome their involvement in their children's education, and that you, as their child's teacher, want to stay in touch with them.

 Early in the first week of school, send a letter home explaining your desire to welcome classroom visitors and volunteers. Tell them about the daily learning log they'll be getting each week. Provide them with the school phone number and let them know a convenient time to reach you. Give parents a list of supplies they'll need to provide, such as a box of tissues, towelettes, a water bottle, and postcards.

 Maintain as much of an open-door policy in your classroom as possible. By welcoming parents, you encourage communication. Decide whether it's necessary for parents to inform you of an upcoming visit or if a "drop-in" visit is acceptable. This will be a personal preference and it may change from year to year. Once you've established a policy, apply it to all of your students' parents.

 If you plan to use volunteers in your room, develop a system to organize work for them to do. A box with a lid can be used to store work. As parents enter the room, they'll get into the habit of checking for work or notes regarding jobs that need to be completed. Some parents prefer to work only with students, while others will be happy to do correcting or other work. Ask how they would like to spend their time and also how they would like the class to address them. Be sure to thank parents for all their help.

 At the start of the school year, inform parents that they'll be getting daily reports on classroom activities. This can be done easily by having your students maintain a learning log or a daily calendar. Instruct students to write (or draw, depending on the grade level) three things they did that day. Encourage parents and students to talk about their activities. Have parents sign the daily calendar or log for students to return to school the next day. Continue this interaction throughout the week. On Fridays, students who have kept track of the calendar all week and have signatures can be rewarded. Rewards might be a sticker, a piece of candy, a coupon for free classroom time, or a spot on a special star-of-the-week chart. The rewards need to be appropriate to the children's age and your teaching style.

Ask parents to provide two stamped postcards addressed to themselves. Write an encouraging note home to parents, praising their child in some way. Choose a time when you can sincerely relate some positive occurrence or behavior. Parents and students love to get these special postcards in the mail.

Send all notices regarding activities or meetings home well in advance of the event. Nothing is more frustrating to a busy parent then to receive a last-minute notice. To be sure parents have received notices, include a section at the bottom for parents to sign, cut off, and return to school. For younger children, offer a sticker to those who return this signature.

 Write a weekly newsletter to be sent home each Friday. Divide the paper into five days of the week. For each day report a memorable event. Include study topics, special events, and projects. Keep a simple format so you will be able to maintain the newsletter through the year.

Once a month take time to write a half-page note to parents, and make a copy for each student. Use a comfortable, easy-to-read style. These notes can be about a special classroom project, upcoming event, or an improved classroom behavior. This reminds parents that they are an important part of their child's classroom.

 A great way to create lasting memories for parents and students is to make individual video recordings of each student. At the beginning of the year, have each child bring in a videotape labeled with his or her name. Whenever a child gives a report or a performance for the class, capture important moments on videotape. It's important to include the entire presentation or report. Explain to the class the need to listen quietly, as any comments or noises will be recorded. When taping is finished, the student may take the videotape home and show it to his or her family. Remind students to rewind tapes at home before watching, but not to rewind when they are finished watching. This way the tape is ready for the next taping. Tapes should be kept at school and only allowed to go home for one night of viewing. Your tapes can be passed on to next year's teacher for more recording, or sent home at the end of the school year as a keepsake.

 Keep a stack of thank-you cards in your desk drawer so you can thank parents when they send in special items such as flowers, treats, or other things of interest to the class. Try to send the note home with the student the same day the time arrives.

 At the beginning of the school year, and when you begin new units of study, it's important to keep parents informed of subjects to be covered. Explain your mode of communication, such as through newsletters and learning logs, to encourage two-way dialogue.

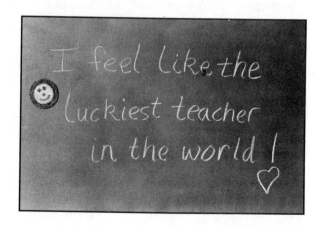

Communicating with Staff

Your colleagues, both teachers and staff members, can be a tremendous resource. Tap into their experience and insight by nurturing an open and friendly relationship. Make a point of knowing staff members' first names and job titles. A smile, a friendly hello, or sincere compliment about a special activity or display takes only a minute but can leave lingering warmth.

 Keep a pad handy to jot down notes regarding special reminders or to just say hello. Using attractive or humorous paper can make the message stand out.

 Use thank-you notes or postcards to express your appreciation. A hand-written note, rather than a printed message, goes a long way toward making someone feel valued.

 Don't be afraid to ask questions. Teachers generally love to share information and will do so readily when asked. Asking

questions is a great way to get to know others. Be willing to share your ideas as well. Offer staff members genuine "listening time" when requested.

 Keep a list of staff members' birthdays (usually available from the school office). Make a point of wishing them a happy birthday or sending a card to celebrate the occasion.

 Create an "Idea Folder" for staff members. Keep the folder in the library or staff room. The "Idea Folder" can be one file folder or several folders, each for a different topic such as teaching reading, art projects, math ideas, or discipline. The front of the folder(s) should be clearly labeled and have several pieces of blank paper inside. Encourage staff members to share their ideas by writing them on the paper. Have them write their names next to their ideas so they receive credit and can be contacted for more information.

CHAPTER EIGHT

Organizing Paperwork

As a teacher you will never be short of paperwork. Not only will you have the paperwork generated by your students, but also paperwork that comes to you from your state educational offices, district offices, parents, clubs, conference networks, and companies you've never heard of.

Filing

You will have highly significant paperwork that requires your attention and focus. You will also have unimportant, redundant, irrelevant paperwork that does not merit your time or attention. Your goal is to know which is which, and to rid yourself of the rest. The best way to do this is to sort and file each paper as it comes to you. Try to avoid stockpiling papers to sort later. It is not only more difficult to sort large piles of paperwork, but it is also more difficult to store. Sorting items as they come to you is not only more efficient, it is habit forming. You will find that you can no longer tolerate large piles of paperwork looming around your classroom waiting to be sorted.

Sort your papers into three categories:

To Be Filed　　**To Be Read**　　**To Be Discarded**

 Papers to be filed will be those that have information you want to keep on hand. This might be state or district information, school information, parent information or teaching tips. These papers can be filed in file folders and kept in your filing cabinet. Several file folders can be pre-marked and awaiting these papers. These folders could be labeled as follows:

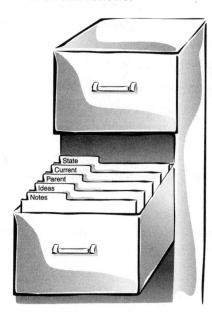

- State/District Information
- State/District Information CURRENT
- Parent/Student Information
- Parent/Student Information CURRENT
- (school name) Information
- (school name) Information CURRENT
- Programs/Courses/Conferences
- Ideas
- Notes and Cards
- Confidential

Folders bearing the label "Current" should contain information received during the current year. When the next school year begins, papers from the current folders should be reviewed. Any of the papers to be saved can be moved into the noncurrent folder. Any information no longer significant should be discarded.

Folders labeled "Programs/Courses/ Conferences" should be reviewed and sorted every few months. Information in this folder can become outdated quickly and needs to be thinned out.

The "Idea Folder" will continue to grow and grow. As it becomes full, sort it into subject areas. Keep a basket or folder at your desk labeled "Ideas to Use Right Away."

A folder labeled "Notes and Cards" should be added to each time you get an endearing note from a student, parent, or colleague. This is a great folder to pull out in those moments when you're overwhelmed and not feeling at your peak. Over the years, you'll enjoy looking back at the messages from those whose lives you've touched.

A folder labeled "Confidential" folder should contain information that has been given to you in confidence or that you feel should be confidential. It may be information from parents or colleagues regarding students, or it may be information about topics you are researching and are not yet ready to share. Keeping the papers in this folder will help you to remember that the information is not to be shared freely.

If your school uses weekly bulletins, they should be kept for the week they are announcing. If they contain information about upcoming events, be sure to mark them on your calendar. Once the week is over, the schedule can be tossed out. If you need to refer to the schedule once the week is over, the office will have a copy of it.

If you have trouble throwing things away, you may prefer a more general filing system which allows you to keep most everything. You can have three folders with the labels:

Significant and Urgent

Significant But Not Urgent

Not Significant

Papers you can't decide how to deal with can be placed in a "Transition Box." This box can be stored in a cupboard where it is not highly visible. Once a paper is put in the "Transition Box" it can be retrieved if it gains importance. If the paper is not missed and gradually fades from your memory, you can then comfortably throw it away.

Absent Work

 Keep a file folder labeled "Absent Work" in a resealable bag. Place the folder on the absent student's desk and place papers in it throughout the day. At the end of the day, the folder will be ready to slip into the resealable bag and sent home. The resealable bag can be decorated with permanent markers and stickers to make it look cheery. Replace both the bag and the file folder every few months depending on how much use it gets. It's a good idea to have at least three folders and bags ready to go in case of multiple absences.

 Students who are absent miss valuable time in the classroom and important class work. In order to keep students up-to-date they need to have information about missed work.

 To help students keep up with classroom work, send home materials in a resealable plastic bag, along with a note such as the example on page 66.

Makeup Assignments

Sorry you are sick. We miss you!
Get Well Soon!

Today's date _____

Work for _____

Math _____

Reading _____

Spelling _____

Social Studies/Science _____

Writing _____

Other _____

Special information: _____

_____

_____

_____

_____

_____

_____

_____

Reproducible

A FINAL NOTE

Organizing a classroom is an evolving process, one that requires constant tinkering and revision. Since student needs and educational trends change from year to year, it's important to periodically step back and re-think about how you organize your classroom—and your expectations.

Revamping the classroom environment is a physical act, requiring a fair amount of housecleaning and repositioning of objects you may not have considered before. But true renovation is more complex than shifting desks and alphabetizing library books: Organizing your classroom begins within you.

Know from the onset that all of your expectations—about teaching, student achievement, parental involvement, and district support—will be tested like you never imagined back in graduate school. Those same early expectations, however unrealistic, have a way of creeping back, influencing the way you interact with students. Beware of the power of preconceived notions and make adjustments, as needed.

It's essential, as you begin to restructure the physical nature of your classroom that you also take time to re-examine your expectations; too high and they may put undue pressure on you and your students; too low and you may lose motivation, inspiring less than a student's best work.

Intially, organizing your classroom may seem like a daunting task. Where do you begin?

 First, be kind to yourself—don't expect changes suggested in this book, or any other for that matter, to occur overnight.

Be patient. Teaching is a demanding profession, requiring a complex combination of artistry, skill, and craftsmanship. You're not going to be able to implement *all* the great ideas you got at a workshop, for example, within the first week, so give yourself a break. Teaching is a process. Good ideas will eventually find their way into your curriculum.

 Second, give yourself time. Allow yourself to fail. Master teachers are masters because of what they've learned along the way. Teaching is a journey that improves with time. Remember to indulge yourself in the same care and loving guidance you freely share with students.

 Third, learn to be flexible. If you're in this profession for the long run, there's no room for rigidity. *Teaching* is a verb that's constantly changing. That same spirit of flexibility also applies to professional relationships—from the school district level down. Instead of seeing administrative paperwork as a burden, try to shift your thinking: The district's in the business of organizing correct procedure so you can be in the business of teaching children.

Finally, as you begin the process of organizing your classroom, know that the suggestions in this book are designed to free your day, not add additional burdens. Toss out the guilt. Bury the "shoulds."

Most importantly, remember to laugh, cry, sing, frown, and smile with your students. Demonstrate your love of learning in everything you do. If you teach from the heart, there's no greater gift you can give them.

EPILOGUE

Fearon Teacher Aids hopes that Katherine Ruggieri's *How to Organize Your Classroom* has inspired you, triggering even more organizational ideas. We'd love to hear from you. Please share your stories, tips, and photographs by writing to:

Fearon Teacher Aids
How to Organize Your Classroom
23740 Hawthorne Blvd.
Torrance, CA 90505-5927